21st Century Junior Library

Spinosaurus

by Josh Gregory

CHERRY LAKE PUBLISHING * ANN ARBOR, MICHIGAN

Published in the United States of America by Cherry Lake Publishing
Ann Arbor, Michigan
www.cherrylakepublishing.com

Content Adviser: Gregory M. Erickson, PhD, Dinosaur Paleontologist, Department of Biological
Science, Florida State University, Tallahassee, Florida

Reading Adviser: Marla Conn, ReadAbility, Inc.

Photo Credits: Cover, ©Stocktrek Images, Inc./Alamy; pages 4 and 18, ©Kostyantyn Ivanyshen/
Shutterstock, Inc.; page 6, ©Linda Bucklin/Shutterstock, Inc.; page 8, ©ExpressionImage/
Shutterstock, Inc.; page 10, ©Sofia Santos/Shutterstock, Inc.; page 12, ©Derrick Neill/
Dreamstime.com; page 14, ©Catmando/Shutterstock, Inc.; page 16, ©iStockphoto.com/
AdrianChesterman; page 20, ©AP Photo/Francois Mori.

LIBRARY OF CONGRESS CATALOGING-IN-PUBLICATION DATA
Gregory, Josh.
  Spinosaurus/by Josh Gregory.
    p. cm.—(21st century junior library. Dinosaurs and prehistoric animals)
  Summary: "Learn about the life, habits, and history of the Spinosaurus"— Provided by publisher.
  Audience: K to grade 3.
  Includes bibliographical references and index.
  ISBN 978-1-62431-164-2 (lib. bdg.)—ISBN 978-1-62431-230-4 (e-book)—
ISBN 978-1-62431-296-0 (pbk.)
  1. Spinosaurus—Juvenile literature. 2. Dinosaurs—Juvenile literature. I. Title.
  QE862.S3G768 2014
  567.912—dc23   2013004933

Cherry Lake Publishing would like to acknowledge the work of
The Partnership for 21st Century Skills.
Please visit www.p21.org for more information.

Printed in the United States of America
Corporate Graphics Inc.
July 2013
CLFA13

CONTENTS

Spinosaurus was a dangerous hunter.

What Was
Spinosaurus?

Picture a massive dinosaur with a sail on its back. You probably imagine something a lot like *Spinosaurus*. *Spinosaurus* lived about 100 million years ago. It may have been the largest meat-eating dinosaur that ever lived. Like all dinosaurs, this incredible hunter is now **extinct**.

Spinosaurus was comfortable both on land and in the water.

Spinosaurus was named for the sail-like shape of its **spine**. The scientist who first discovered *Spinosaurus* **fossils** gave this creature its name. This amazing dinosaur lived in what is now North Africa. It spent time on land and in the water.

Look!

Look up some pictures of other dinosaurs. Do any of them look like *Spinosaurus*? What do they have in common?

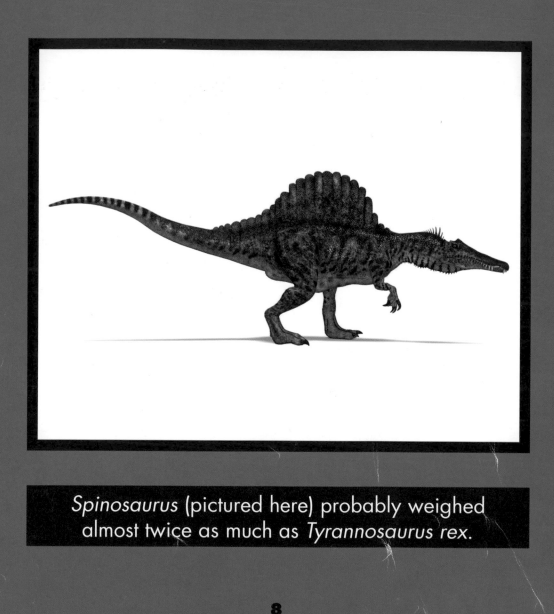

Spinosaurus (pictured here) probably weighed almost twice as much as *Tyrannosaurus rex.*

What Did *Spinosaurus* Look Like?

Spinosaurus was a huge dinosaur. It was between 46 and 59 feet (14 and 18 meters) long. *Spinosaurus* was also very heavy. It weighed between 13 and 22 tons (12,000 and 20,000 kilograms). That is longer and heavier than a school bus!

Some scientists argue that *Spinosaurus*'s spine was colorful.

Spinosaurus is famous for its spiny sail. This sail could be almost 6 feet (2 m) tall. Scientists aren't sure what it was used for. *Spinosaurus* may have used it to find a mate. It may also have scared away enemies. Some scientists think the spine was actually a hump. The dinosaur would have stored fat there for energy.

Spinosaurus's long, narrow mouth was probably great for catching fish.

Spinosaurus had very long jaws. Its **skull** was about 5.5 feet (1.7 m) long. The jaws were lined with pointy teeth. The front teeth were longer than those in back.

Create! Try drawing a picture of *Spinosaurus*. Include its spiny sail and long mouth. What else can you add to make your drawing look real?

*Spinosaurus*es probably spent most of their time on two legs.

Spinosaurus had sharp claws. Its legs were longer than its arms. Experts think it stood on its back legs in the water. It used its tail to balance when standing on two legs. *Spinosaurus* sometimes rested on all fours when on land.

Scientists believe fish were a large part of
Spinosaurus's diet.

How Did
Spinosaurus Live?

Spinosaurus probably did not have many **predators**. It was too large for most other dinosaurs to kill it. It was free to hunt food with few worries. *Spinosaurus* probably ate giant fish. It may have also hunted small dinosaurs.

Spinosaurus may have hunted smaller dinosaurs on land.

Spinosaurus was big and heavy. But it could still move fast. Scientists estimate that it reached speeds of 12 to 15 miles (19 to 24 kilometers) per hour. This is about as fast as most humans can run. *Spinosaurus*'s speed may have helped it chase down **prey**.

Spinosaurus skeletons at museums are built using a a mix of fossils from many different *Spinosaruses.*

Spinosaurus fossils were first found in Egypt in North Africa in 1912. Very few *Spinosaurus* remains have been discovered since then. Some fossils have been found in other North African countries. *Spinosaurus* fossils can be seen in museums around the world.

Make a Guess!

How are fossils formed? How do scientists uncover them? Try looking for the answers in a book. Your teacher or librarian can help you find the right book.

GLOSSARY

extinct (ik-STINGKT) describing a type of plant or animal that has completely died out

fossils (FAH-suhlz) the preserved remains of living things from thousands or millions of years ago

predators (PRED-uh-turz) animals that live by hunting other animals for food

prey (PRAY) an animal that is hunted by other animals for food

skull (SKUHL) the bones that make up an animal's head

spine (SPINE) backbone

FIND OUT MORE

BOOKS

Dixon, Dougal. *Spinosaurus and Other Dinosaurs of Africa.* Minneapolis: Picture Window Books, 2007.

Gray, Susan H. *Spinosaurus.* Mankato, MN: Child's World, 2010.

WEB SITES

Discovery—Monsters Resurrected: Spinosaurus Killing Style
http://dsc.discovery.com /video-topics/other/dinosaur-videos/monsters-resurrected-spinosaurus-killing-style.htm
Watch a video showing what *Spinosaurus* may have looked like.

Spinosaurus: The Largest Carnivorous Dinosaur
www.livescience.com /24120-spinosaurus.html
Look at useful diagrams to learn more about *Spinosaurus*.

INDEX

ABOUT THE AUTHOR

Josh Gregory writes and edits books for kids. He lives in Chicago, Illinois.